NEW PERSPECTIVES

Chernobyl and other Nuclear Accidents

JUDITH CONDON

WAYLAND

First published in 1998 by
Wayland Publishers Ltd,
61 Western Road,
Hove,
East Sussex BN3 1JD

This book was prepared for Wayland Publishers Ltd
by Ruth Nason.

Series editor: Alex Woolf
Series design: Stonecastle Graphics
Book design: LNbooks, Houghton Regis, Bedfordshire

Find Wayland on the internet at:
http://www.wayland.co.uk

British Library Cataloguing in Publication Data
Condon, Judith
  Chernobyl and other nuclear accidents. – (New
  perspectives)
  1. Chernobyl Nuclear Accident, Chernobyl', Ukraine,
  1986 – Juvenile literature. 2. Nuclear power plants –
  Accidents – Juvenile literature
  I. Title
  363.1'799'09477

ISBN 0 7502 2170 4

Printed and bound in Italy by G. Canale & C.S.p.A., Turin

Acknowledgements

The Author thanks Chris Bryer and Yorkshire Television/Channel 4
for permission to quote from *Children of Chernobyl*; Sita Guneratne;
and Laurie Flynn, to whom enormous thanks are due.

The Author and Publishers thank the following for their permission
to reproduce photographs: Camera Press: p. 52; Cornelia Hesse-
Honegger: p. 59; JVZ Picture Library: pp. 5b, 22, 57b; Novosti: pp. 1,
7, 9, 10, 13, 14, 15, 16, 56; Popperfoto: pp. 3, 4, 20b, 23, 28b, 29, 31,
32, 33, 38t, 47, 51b; Rex Features Ltd: pp. 19, 57t; Science Photo
Library: cover (foreground) and pp. 20t, 28t, 34, 42, 43, 45, 49, 54, 55;
Society for Cooperation in Russian and Soviet Studies: pp. 12t, 17,
18; Topham Picturepoint: cover (background) and pp. 12b, 21, 25,
26, 27, 37, 38b, 39, 40, 41, 46, 48, 51t, 53.

Cover photos: Protective radiation suits worn by decontamination operators at Three Mile Island; a view of Unit 4 of the Chernobyl nuclear power plant, three days after the accident in April 1986.

Page 1: Cleaning up a building in a Soviet town contaminated by radiation.

CONTENTS

April 1996: ten years after the accident at Chernobyl, a worker takes a reading of radioactivity inside the sarcophagus built over the damaged reactor.

CATASTROPHE AT CHERNOBYL

In the middle of the night of Friday, 25 - Saturday, 26 April 1986, the reactor in Unit 4 of the Chernobyl Nuclear Power Station was being prepared for shutdown. This was a routine procedure, enabling maintenance and repairs to be carried out. It had been decided to use the opportunity to conduct a series of tests on the unit's turbines. Anatoli Dyatlov, deputy chief engineer of Unit 4, was on hand, and Gennady Matlenko had come from the equipment manufacturers. Several Chernobyl engineers had also gathered in the control room, hoping to learn.

The control room of Reactor 3 at Chernobyl Nuclear Power Station, ten years after the accident at Reactor 4.

At the main control board stood Alexander Akimov, the shift foreman, and 26-year-old engineer Leonid Toptunov. As they scanned the complicated dials and gauges, they were nervous. Normally, emergency systems would come into operation automatically if anything went wrong in the reactor. But because the tests might make it appear that something was wrong, those automatic emergency systems had been turned off. Akimov and Toptunov had the great responsibility of watching to see that the reactor stayed within control.

The Soviet Union was chronically short of electricity. That is why the power station at Chernobyl had been built at such speed, and the new town of Pripyat had sprung up to house its workers. Unit 4 had begun operating in March 1984, without time for certain tests

00085022.

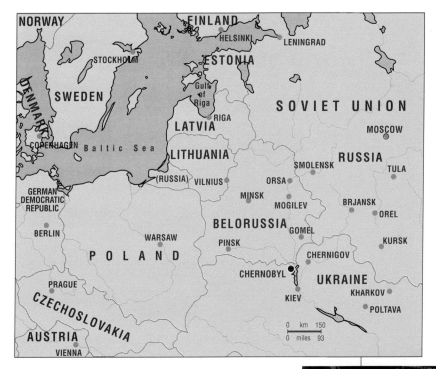

Above: Chernobyl is in Ukraine, which, in 1986, was a republic of the Soviet Union. Ukraine became independent in 1991.

Right: The hall above Reactor 3 at the Chernobyl Nuclear Power Station. Reactor 4 was identical to this.

to be carried out. It was crucial to the electric power grid at Kiev, the country's third largest city. That very Friday an order to postpone shut-down had arrived – after the procedure had started – because Unit 4's output was urgently needed. Late at night, permission to resume the procedure had finally been given.

Shut-down involves lowering control rods into the core of a reactor (see page 30) to reduce its power to a minimum. Around midnight, Akimov and Toptunov realized that the power of the reactor had sunk too low for the tests to go ahead. All their training told them it would now be best to shut down the reactor and abandon the tests.

But Dyatlov, their superior, became impatient. The tests on the turbines had already been postponed once. He blamed the men's incompetence and ordered the control rods to be withdrawn immediately to increase power. Reluctantly Akimov and Toptunov obeyed. By 1 a.m. power had risen just high enough for the tests on the turbines to start.

Seconds later, it was clear to the operators that things were going badly wrong. There was an enormous surge of power. Water flow through the reactor core increased, putting pressure on the pumps and causing vibrations in the pipes. They tried to adjust matters, but it was hard to know what was happening.

At 1.23 a.m. the dials indicated a dangerous surge in power and radiation. Akimov shouted to Dyatlov that he was going to push the emergency AZ button to lower all the control rods into the core. There were several loud thuds. The descending control rods had jammed. Simultaneously there was a terrible tremor, described afterwards as being like an earthquake.

Reactor number 4 had exploded. The force of the explosion was so great that it blew the 2,000-tonne steel lid off the top of the core, and dislodged the concrete outer shield. A huge fire followed.

'It was a nuclear explosion'

Lila Sipkina, a nurse at the local hospital, described the moment when the reactor exploded:

'That night I was on duty at the hospital. Suddenly there was ... a loud explosion. For a moment everything went black. I couldn't understand what was happening. The sky was lit up. Those lights, it was like in a fairy tale. Suddenly I realized I'd seen something like it ... on television when they show how they launch sputniks. It was a nuclear explosion ... a nuclear mushroom.'
(From *Children of Chernobyl*, TV documentary)

Firefighters risk their lives

Boris Aleshaev, one of the first firefighters to arrive on the scene, recalled:

'As we approached we could see the reactor was burning ... The roof was on fire. Parts of the wall had collapsed. Everywhere it was burning ... When we arrived at the site we saw some shapeless pieces with a hole in the middle. One chap said it was graphite from the reactor which meant the core was destroyed. The radiation levels must be high – it must be dangerous. Some people came and kicked it away to stop it setting fire to the car tyres. It was hot. The tarmac was melting under it. One lad even picked some up to see what it was. He is no longer with us – he died.' (From *Children of Chernobyl*, TV documentary)

As yet none of those on duty believed this had happened. In the confusion, men were sent off through dark wrecked passageways. Two were told to try to lower the rods manually – an impossibility. Others were sent to try to turn the huge valves of the emergency cooling system, knee-deep in radioactive water. Four men climbed from the 12th to the 35th level, and looked down. It was like looking into the crater of a burning volcano.

This photograph of Reactor 4 was taken from a helicopter in May 1986.

Firefighters arrived and battled heroically to prevent the fire spreading to Unit 3. With no special protective clothing, they climbed the outer stairways and directed their hoses at the burning roof of the turbine hall. The bitumen was melting under their feet, ignited by chunks of black burning graphite from the reactor core. After a short while, many began to feel ill and were carried away.

The effects of radiation begin to show

The instrument used to measure radiation is called a dosimeter. After reactor 4 exploded, the levels of radiation were so high they went off the top of the scale. Many firefighters were led or carried away, beginning to suffer from the effects of their exposure. Boris Aleshaev remembered:

'They started measuring the radiation but it was too high. It was coming from us – dust, bits of graphite that were on us. One dosimetrist came up and said, "What am I meant to measure? The meter's gone off the scale." I started to feel very tired. I felt sick. I wanted to lie down and have a rest – forget about everything. My body and face were glowing. People began to lose consciousness. They started vomiting and were taken to hospital.' (From *Children of Chernobyl*, TV documentary)

At the hospital there were not enough beds. People were put on the floor.

By 4 a.m. fire crews were arriving from Kiev, 100 kilometres away, and by 5 a.m. the fire on the roof had been brought under control. A security cordon had been placed around the Chernobyl complex, and guards checked everyone going in or out. The Soviet Union was a society where people were used to obeying orders from officialdom. No one felt authorized to shut down the other reactors. No one decided on an evacuation. No one warned the people of Pripyat. At the other three reactors, shifts of workers arrived and left as normal. At Unit 5, still under construction, building work did not stop. With daylight came a message: a government commission had been appointed and would arrive later that day. Meanwhile, avoid panic!

At 10 a.m. on Saturday a team of experts arrived from Moscow. It was estimated that the temperature in the reactor core was at least 2,500 degrees Centigrade. The core might go on burning for weeks or months. It was decided to try to smother the fire with sacks of sand dropped from helicopters. The sand would be mixed with lead, boron and dolomite, to try to block the radiation which was rising in vapour from the inferno.

Men rushed to commandeer supplies, including sand from the river banks. In the next few days hundreds of helicopter sorties were made, at great risk to the pilots. They had to fly low enough to hit their target, while avoiding the many pylons and tall chimneys. They suffered in the intense heat that rose from the core, and were given iodine pills to counteract the effects of radiation.

A helicopter is tested for radioactive contamination after flying over Chernobyl.

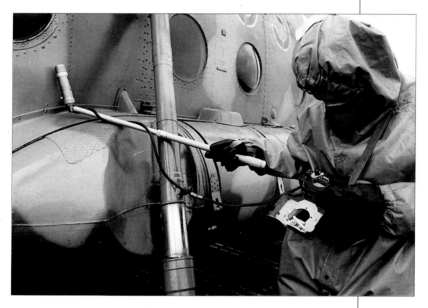

Locally and nationally, there was a total news blackout. Throughout Saturday morning rumours circulated in Pripyat, as word reached families about fathers and husbands taken to hospital. But most people were not alarmed. The weather was unusually warm. They were happily making plans for the 1 May holiday. They went about their shopping or took younger children to the park.

Older children were at school as normal. In the middle of the afternoon a message went out to schools to close their windows as a precaution, but still there was no public warning.

It was not until Sunday morning that an official announcement was made, that the town's inhabitants were to be evacuated. Hundreds of buses were ready waiting. From the early afternoon 50,000 people, including 17,000 children, carrying a few hastily packed belongings, began to board. Most thought they would be away from Pripyat for two or three days. In fact, they were never to return.

A guard stands at the barrier to keep people out of the exclusion zone set up around Chernobyl.

 The first official announcement, Sunday, 27 April 1986

Newsreel recorded the words that came from loudspeakers across Pripyat:

'Attention. Attention. Honourable comrades! Following an accident at the Chernobyl nuclear power station an unfavourable radiation situation is arising in the town of Pripyat. Today, 27 April, beginning at 1400 hours, it will be necessary to start a temporary evacuation of the town's inhabitants to nearby settlements in the Kiev region.'

Evacuated ... but not to safety

Buses full of evacuees from Pripyat began to arrive in Polesskoe, 48 kilometres from Chernobyl. In fact, the town lay directly in the path of the radioactive plume carried on the wind and so it and the surrounding forest were already highly contaminated. Olga Yanchuk, a teacher, lived in a flat in Polesskoe. She remembers:

'On the Sunday night a lot of buses came into town. They asked us to take in people from Pripyat. We didn't think it was serious. But the head of the district committee lives across the hall. I saw him and the prosecutor take their children away in the middle of the night. You understand? I had three small children so I asked, "Give me a travel pass so that I too can get out of here." And they said to me, "Everything is normal here."' (From *Children of Chernobyl*, TV documentary)

On Monday, 28 April, 1,600 kilometres to the north, monitors in Sweden detected high levels of radiation. At first it was assumed that there had been a Soviet nuclear weapons test. But analysis showed that the radionuclides (radioactive atoms) were from a nuclear reactor. When Swedish diplomats urgently contacted Moscow, they received only denials. Finally, the Soviet authorities realized that they could no longer hide the truth. At 9 p.m. – the end of the third day – a statement was issued to the world by the official Soviet news agency TASS. The same statement was broadcast on Moscow television's news programme 'Vremya'.

'An accident has occurred'

At 9 p.m. on 28 April the government news agency TASS announced what had happened:

'An accident has occurred at the Chernobyl atomic power plant. One of the atomic reactors has been damaged. Measures are being undertaken to eliminate the consequences of the accident. Aid is being given to those affected. A government commission has been set up.'

Workers parade in Kiev,
1 May 1986.

On 1 May the annual May Day parades went ahead in Moscow and Kiev. Crowds of people were on the streets enjoying the sunshine. But the danger was far from over. For one thing, the emission of radionuclides from the burning reactor started to increase again. What was happening? Had smothering the fire caused it to become hotter? Could it be burning downwards, through the concrete base? Below, it might react with water to produce an explosion even greater than the first one. Three men went on a dangerous mission to check conditions below the reactor. Then another three men dived into highly radioactive water to open valves to drain the bubbler pool, a large water reserve beneath the reactor.

Ukraine, 1987: measuring people's radioactivity.

On 6 May radionuclide emissions suddenly decreased. On 7 May the pumping out of contaminated water from the flooded basement was completed. On 9 May the fire was still visible but, after a further 80 tonnes of lead had been dropped the next day, the glow ceased.

At great human cost the fire had been prevented from spreading to other reactors in the Chernobyl complex, and the danger of a second explosion had been averted. However, no one could foresee the long-term human, political and environmental repercussions of the disaster at Chernobyl.

The human cost

Official accounts of the accident at Chernobyl state that 31 people died. But scientist Z. A. Medvedev writes that troops and air force personnel were taken to military hospitals, and their casualties not disclosed.

Among the first victims were the two operators, Alexander Akimov and Leonid Toptunov. Although ordered to leave, and showing signs of radiation sickness, they went to try to turn the valves to bring water to the core. A few days later, in hospital in Moscow, their skin turned dark and their flesh began to disintegrate. Radioactive vapour had burned their lungs so they had trouble breathing. Their bodies were still highly radioactive. In spite of bone marrow transplants their internal organs were disintegrating too. Akimov talked to Razim Davetbayev, who visited him in his sterile room.

"'My chances are slim," he said to Razim, and to prove it he pulled out a tuft of his hair. "But if I do survive, one thing is for sure: I'll never go back to work in the nuclear field. I'll do anything ... I'll start my life from scratch,

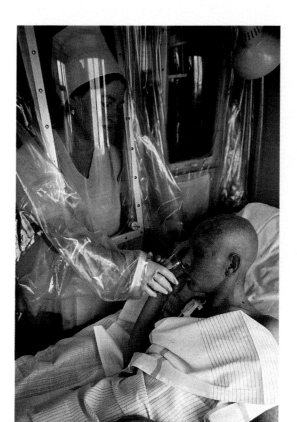

but I'll never go back to reactors."' (Quoted in Read, *Ablaze*)

Akimov died on 10 May and Toptunov died on 14 May 1986. In the cemetery, special concrete slabs were placed under their coffins, and those of other victims, to prevent radionuclides from seeping into the soil.

Thousands of others caught up in the emergency received high doses of radiation that would cause severe illness, and shorten their lives, in the months and years to come.

August 1986: a nurse at a Moscow hospital tends a victim of the Chernobyl accident whose body is still highly radioactive.

THE FALL-OUT SPREADS

Once the immediate danger of a second explosion had been averted, the Soviet authorities had to tackle the enormous problem of cleaning up after the accident and trying to prevent radioactive contamination from spreading further.

To protect them from radiation, men involved in the clean-up put on aprons of soft lead underneath overalls of rubberized lead.

At Unit 4, the graphite had burned out, and the temperature of the reactor core had declined to about 270 degrees Centigrade, but the condition of the nuclear fuel inside was not known. Moreover, lumps of graphite and uranium had been spewed out by the explosion across a wide area, including the roof of Unit 3. Aerial photographs showed glowing spots where fragments of nuclear fuel had been cast on the ground. These were covered with concrete by remote-controlled bulldozers flown in by transport aircraft. The highly radioactive graphite on the roof posed a more difficult problem. Mobile robots bought from Germany proved unable to function on the melted bitumen of the roof. The only answer was to use humans.

It was calculated that, in protective clothing, a person could spend between one and two minutes on the roof before accumulating the maximum dose of radiation considered allowable for a whole lifetime. Young soldiers and men press-ganged for the purpose were sent up the staircase leading to the roof. One after the other they ran with a shovel, scooped up the

Pets and wildlife suffered too

Some 600,000 people were involved in the clean-up of the zone around Chernobyl. Nikolai Goshchitsky was among them. Early in June 1986, he visited the abandoned town of Pripyat and later described seeing hundreds of birds and animals, either dead or blind.

'When they remembered about the animals, they began to shoot them – kindness demanded it ... they crawled, half alive, along the road, in terrible pain. Birds looked as if they had crawled out of water, unable to fly or walk. Cats with dirty fur, as if it had been burnt in places.' (Quoted in Medvedev, *The Legacy of Chernobyl*)

radioactive fragments, rushed to the edge and threw them into the abyss of the burned-out shell of Unit 4, then hurried to take cover behind a concrete wall. Even though they were given protective clothing, the men feared for themselves, and for any children they might have in the future, because of the genetic damage likely to be caused by the radiation. The danger came not only from the graphite and uranium, but from dust that now covered the whole area, including the abandoned town of Pripyat.

A large swathe of forest was singed brown; wildlife and domestic animals lay dead, or foraged weakly for food. There was no simple solution to such widespread contamination. Trees were felled but could not be burned because the smoke and ash would be radio-active. In the months that followed, vast pits were dug and lined with concrete. Into them were pitched contaminated trees, vehicles and topsoil.

Machinery used in the clean-up awaits burial.

The worst fear was that contamination would be washed into streams feeding the Pripyat and Dnieper rivers. The Kiev Sea and the waters of the Dnieper, on its way to the Black Sea, supply drinking water to fifty million people. Rain was forecast, so time was short. In just over a week – a seemingly impossible timescale – a subterranean wall was built between the reactor and the Pripyat river to contain radioactive ground water.

The sarcophagus

Reactor 4 itself was to be encased in a huge steel and concrete shell, or sarcophagus, designed to contain radiation. Because it was feared that the core of the reactor would burn down into the earth's crust, miners and underground railway workers, without protective clothing, tunnelled beneath the foundations. Liquid nitrogen was pumped into the soil to freeze it solid. By the end of June 1986 a huge concrete cushion was also in place beneath the reactor.

Above ground, steel tanks measuring 18 by 6 by 6 metres were hauled into position and filled with concrete to make the giant bricks of a massive wall behind which construction workers could shelter from radiation emitted by the remains of reactor 4. Then work on the sarcophagus itself began. Its walls at the base were 8 metres thick; the concrete struts were 55 metres high. Huge girders were stretched across the top and covered in concrete to seal the roof. By the end of September, the giant tomb was complete.

The spreading effects

The accident at Chernobyl had exposed people to radiation between 100 and 200 times greater than that from the

The sarcophagus, May 1987.

Evacuees, 1986.

explosion of the Hiroshima atomic bomb. At first, a 10-kilometre exclusion zone had been established around the Chernobyl complex. This was extended on 2 May 1986 to 30 kilometres, and further evacuations took place. Thousands of children were sent away to summer camps. Many old people resisted leaving their homes, unable to understand the nature of the calamity that had overtaken them.

 ## 'In my dreams every night I return ...'

135,000 people were evacuated from the 30-kilometre zone, and then thousands of others from contaminated areas outside that zone. Anna and her children were evacuated from a village called Slobada in the Bragin region. She described the pain of losing her home:

'Our village had become poisoned too. They told us they would make it better and we would return three days later. But we never returned ... My God you should just see that beautiful place we left. In my dreams every night I return with my family to our home. The river, the trees, our garden, our house and land ... Many of the old people return. They prefer to die of radiation than to die of a broken heart ...' (Quoted in Roche, *Children of Chernobyl: the human cost of the world's worst nuclear disaster*)

High fences and warning signs were set in place around the exclusion zone, but in fact a part of the Soviet Union nearly as large as the whole of Western Europe had been affected. Ukraine and Belorussia were two of the worst-hit regions.

Much of the population of those parts of the Soviet Union lived in far-flung rural villages, working on farms and consuming local produce. They delivered food direct to Kiev – a city of three million inhabitants – and to other nearby towns. Each year in April and May there is a shortage of fresh vegetables, while winter fodder and hay have run out and animals are turned into the fields to graze. Following the Chernobyl accident, there was severe contamination of milk and dairy products, meat, and leafy vegetables. Mushrooms gathered in the forests were also highly contaminated. The Soviet Union did not have a surplus of food on which to draw, and the authorities were faced with immediate shortages.

Restrictions were placed on the sale of local dairy produce in Kiev, but only after 1 May. Restrictions on meat and some leafy vegetables came later. Inevitably, people in the villages went on eating their own produce since they had nothing else.

As reports came in of contamination far beyond the 30-kilometre zone, including vast tracts northeast of Gomel in Belorussia, some areas were evacuated and others were supplied with uncontaminated milk and food. Yet there was dispute and confusion as to what levels of radiation were allowable, and the communist authorities withheld what information they had. They feared widespread panic if it became known that land 300 kilometres north of Chernobyl was uninhabitable, or that deposits of radioactive caesium had been found to the west, just 200

The notice on the tree reads: 'Radioactive Danger Zone! Cattle pasture, haymaking, mushroom- and berry-picking prohibited!'

Contaminated food

Nikolai Kaminsky worked in the meat market in Korosten, a city in Ukraine. He described conditions after the accident:

'Contaminated meat would come into the factory. The internal organs of the cattle would be black and rotten, but still the meat was sold.' (Quoted in *SAGA Magazine*, June 1997)

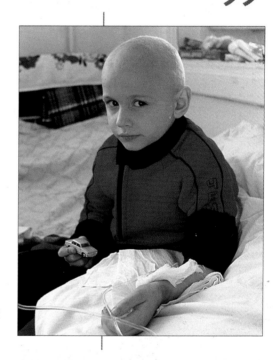

kilometres from Moscow. Maps showing contamination outside the exclusion zone were not made public until 1989.

In Kiev, where the 1 May parades had gone ahead as normal, it was belatedly decided to close all schools early and send children to summer camps. Unborn babies and children are especially vulnerable to the adverse health effects of radiation, and thousands had already been exposed during the public holiday. The children returned to the city when schools reopened in September.

April 1990: a six-year-old victim of the accident at Chernobyl undergoes chemotherapy.

 A child falls ill

Zhana Vlasova and her daughter live in Kiev. Interviewed for British television in 1996, Zhana explained what had happened since the accident:

'It started in 1988 ... when she returned from camp. She went there with hair as long as this. And when she came back I could see a bald patch. Well, we put some cream on. It still kept falling out. I cut her hair short and still it kept falling out. I got afraid. We put her in hospital in November 1988. By the 15th she was completely bald. Completely. Even her eyebrows. She has absolutely no hair on her body. Just imagine – it's awful. She's 14. Her life is just beginning.' (*Children of Chernobyl*, TV documentary)

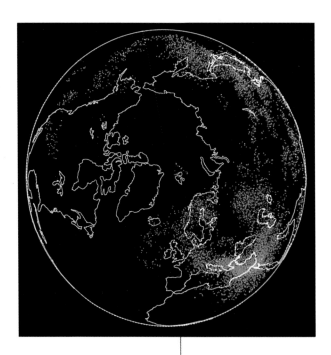

A computer simulation of the spread of radioactivity ten days after the accident at Chernobyl.

Into Europe

The wind that had first alerted monitors in Sweden to the accident had turned south and west on 29 April, carrying radioactive fall-out to almost all countries in Europe. Sweden had been badly hit – especially the northern reindeer territory. Next were Poland, where iodine tablets (to protect against thyroid damage) were given to millions of children, and Germany and Austria. In many countries, huge quantities of milk and leafy vegetables were ordered to be destroyed.

Contamination appeared at a greater distance days later, when rain brought down radioactive particles of caesium and iodine from the high clouds. Upland grazing areas in Wales, northern England and Scotland were among the places affected. Restrictions were placed on the sale of lamb, and on the movement of animals. Some of these restrictions were still in place a decade later.

Scotland, April 1996. This farmer's new lambs must still be tested for signs of radioactive poisoning.

Investigation

The leader of the Soviet Union, Mikhail Gorbachev, promised that the entire truth would be told to the world once the accident had been analysed – an extraordinary development in itself. Since coming to power in 1985, Gorbachev had been steering the Soviet leadership towards 'glasnost', a policy of openness, though this had barely begun to filter down through the channels of the ruling Communist Party.

Soviet leader Mikhail Gorbachev visits the power station at Chernobyl, 1989.

Immediately after the accident, an inquiry into its causes was set up. It became clear that individuals at the power station would be blamed for breaking rules. No serious criticism was to be made of the reactor's design. If the design was blamed, public opinion at home and abroad might force the closure of all similar reactors, with unthinkable consequences for the Soviet economy. The inquiry's findings were followed in July 1987 by the prosecution of the people held responsible, including deputy chief engineer Dyatlov, director Victor Brukhanov and chief engineer Nikolai Fomin. Each was sentenced to ten years in prison.

The court gives its verdict

The trial of individuals held responsible for the accident took place in the town of Chernobyl itself. It was summertime, and hot and dusty. There were pans of water at the entrance to every building, where people were supposed to wash the soles of their shoes, and the lawyers were advised to shower twice a day. On 27 July 1987 the verdict was announced:

'The legal college finds that the defendants Brukhanov, Fomin, Dyatlov, Rogozhkin and Kovalenko are guilty of violations of discipline and regulations guaranteeing safety at plants where there is a potential danger of nuclear explosion, thereby causing human injury and other grievous consequences, in complete contravention of Article 220, Section 2, of the Criminal Code.'

Gorbachev analyses the underlying causes

Mikhail Gorbachev's speech to the Politburo on 3 July 1986 addressed the underlying causes of the accident. He attacked the closed nature and secrecy of the Soviet Union's nuclear power industry, as well as the bureaucracy and narrow thinking of its scientific and political leaders:

'For thirty years you scientists, specialists and ministers have been telling us that everything was safe. And you think that we will look on you as gods. But now we have ended up with a fiasco. The ministers and scientific centres have been working outside of any controls. Throughout the entire system there has reigned a spirit of servility, fawning, clannishness and persecution of independent thinkers, window dressing, and personal and clan ties between leaders.' (Quoted in *Memoirs*)

The abandoned town of Pripyat, photographed in October 1995.

The consequences

The accident at Chernobyl and its aftermath tested the Soviet system to breaking point. Aside from the human suffering, the clean-up cost billions of rubles, to which must be added the cost of long-term medical treatment and re-settlement, and the loss of production caused by reduced power generation. So great was the need for electricity that the other three units at the Chernobyl power station continued production. There was no question of the Soviet Union being able to compensate other countries that had been affected by the accident.

Other nations sent doctors, experts and equipment. For the first time in Soviet history, records of technology and details of an accident were put before the international scientific community in reports to the International Atomic Energy Agency (IAEA) in 1986 and 1987. Even so, secret protocols signed by the Politburo restricted the information released.

The political consequences were momentous. The accident at Chernobyl was part of what broke people's faith in uncontrolled science and an undemocratic system. Within just a few years Central and Eastern Europe underwent huge political changes; Gorbachev was overtaken by the political forces his reforms had helped to unleash; and the Soviet Union ceased to exist.

April 1997: artists in Ukraine stage an anti-nuclear protest on the 11th anniversary of the accident.

The end of the Soviet Union

In his *Memoirs*, published in 1995, Mikhail Gorbachev reflected on the consequences of the Chernobyl explosion:

'Chernobyl shed light on many of the sicknesses of our system as a whole. Everything that had built up over the years converged in this drama: the concealing or hushing up of accidents and other bad news, irresponsibility and carelessness, slipshod work, wholesale drunkenness. This was one more convincing argument in favour of radical reforms.

'The accident at the Chernobyl nuclear power station was graphic evidence, not only of how obsolete our technology was, but also of the failure of the old system. At the same time, and such is the irony of history, it severely affected our reforms by literally knocking the country off its tracks.'

NUCLEAR ENERGY AND THE COLD WAR

The story of the use of nuclear energy dates back to the Second World War, when Britain, the USA and Canada (the Western Allies) raced to produce a nuclear bomb before Hitler's Nazi Germany could do the same. At the end of 1941, US President Roosevelt launched the Manhattan Project. Its aim was to turn the recent discovery of nuclear fission and chain reactions to the purpose of making a bomb capable of winning the war. The project was based at Los Alamos, a remote corner of the state of New Mexico. Here, in utmost secrecy, an international team of scientists conducted research, while plants in Oak Ridge, Tennessee, and Hanford, Washington State, produced the enriched uranium and plutonium to fuel the weapons.

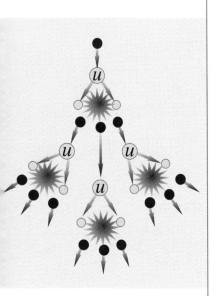

Nuclear fission means the splitting of the nucleus of an atom. Fission can be made to happen by bombarding an atom with a neutron. The atom splits, releasing energy and more neutrons, which go on to bombard other atoms in a chain reaction.

Opposite: CND stands for the Campaign for Nuclear Disarmament, which was founded in Britain in 1958. CND's symbol is based on the semaphore signals for N and D.

Nazi Germany surrendered on 7 May 1945, but Japan fought on against the Western Allies in the Pacific, and as summer advanced, the fighting reached its most desperate stage. The Soviet leader Stalin had promised to commit his forces to the war against Japan, but Harry Truman, who had become US president when Roosevelt died in April, secretly hoped that the atomic bomb would be ready for use before this happened. Although the three countries had been allies since 1941, Britain and the USA now saw the Soviet Union as a menacing rival. At Los Alamos, the race to produce a nuclear bomb did not cease.

The first test bomb was exploded in the New Mexican desert in July 1945, and in August, nuclear bombs were dropped by the US Air Force on the Japanese cities of Hiroshima and Nagasaki. The bombs killed between 100,000 and 200,000 people. Within days, Japan surrendered and the Second World War ended.

The arms race begins

The USA emerged from the Second World War the strongest, wealthiest nation on earth, having previously suffered its worst ever economic depression. 300,000 US troops had been killed, but the gearing of US industry to the production of arms and military equipment had brought about an economic transformation. In the Soviet Union, by comparison, between 15 and 20 million people had died, and vast areas lay in ruins.

Some historians argue that it suited the USA to stoke up fear of Soviet ambition, in order to justify the growth of a highly profitable arms economy. Having already suffered so much from foreign aggression, the Soviet Union was bound to join the race to try to counter American supremacy.

The scientist Albert Einstein had no illusions about the Soviet system's brutality in dealing with its own people. But he held US policy responsible for the drift towards militarization. In letters in 1948 he wrote:

'... it is totally unlikely that any country will attack America in the near future, least of all Russia, which is devastated, impoverished and politically isolated.'

'... the United States is responsible for the ominous competitive arms race which has taken place since the end of the war and which has virtually destroyed the postwar prospects for an effective supranational solution of the security problem.'

The new world scene

As its forces liberated eastern Europe from the Nazis, the Soviet Union extended its influence – and this worried the Western Allies, who feared and distrusted the Soviet communist system. The USA and the Soviet Union now became the main players in a 'Cold War' between 'Western' nations and the 'communist bloc'. It seemed clear that having nuclear weapons would give a nation the potential to dominate the world.

On this new world stage, Britain felt itself being pushed to the side. The Second World War had left it battered and with its empire fading. As a key partner in the Manhattan Project, it had assumed that it would continue to share in the USA's bomb-building programme. But Truman had decided that the USA alone should hold this power.

A British bomb

Consequently, at the end of 1945, Clement Attlee, British prime minister in a newly elected Labour government, decided that Britain should build a nuclear bomb of its own. The project was to be overseen by a secret cabinet committee, under the guidance of Sir Edward Bridges, a high-ranking civil servant, and Sir John Anderson, a Conservative member of Churchill's wartime cabinet. Members of Attlee's cabinet were kept in the dark about the project and it was not discussed in parliament. Some historians say that this secretive decision caused vast amounts of money to be spent on keeping Britain a world power instead of on post-war reconstruction;

Clement Attlee was prime minister of Britain from 1945 to 1951.

Sir John Cockcroft

Dr (later Sir) John Cockcroft was a Nobel prize-winning British scientist. In 1932 he and E.T.S. Watson, working in the Cavendish Laboratory in Cambridge, were the first to 'split' the atom. In 1943 Cockcroft went to Canada, to assist in the Manhattan Project. After the war he was recalled to Britain to head atomic research.

Following a visit to the USA in 1948, where he learned that irradiated particles were being discovered on land around the reactor at Oak Ridge, Cockcroft insisted that filters to trap such particles be fitted to the chimneys at the new British plant at Windscale (see right). But as the chimneys were already half-built, the filter galleries were installed not at the bottom but at the top. (This meant hauling up 200 tonnes of steel, plus bricks, concrete and heavy equipment for each chimney.) At this height, the filters were hard to maintain and later emissions showed that they were not effective. The odd-shaped filter galleries became known as Cockcroft's Follies. **99**

A parliamentary question

'George Jeger MP: "Can the Minister give any further information on the development of nuclear weapons?"

A.V. Alexander, Minister of Defence: "No, I do not think it would be in the public interest to do that."' (House of Commons proceedings, May 1948)

and that Britain's best scientists were diverted from more socially useful research and development.

Under the control of the Ministry of Supply, which had organized Britain's ordnance factories during the war, installations to enrich uranium were sited at Springfields, near Preston, and at Capenhurst, near Chester. Plutonium – enough to make fifteen bombs a year – was to be made at a third site. The place chosen was a disused munitions factory on the coast of Cumbria, at a remote spot called Windscale.

The building of Windscale was a huge project, involving nearly 5,000 workers, including 300 architects, engineers and surveyors. Each of the two reactors weighed 57,000 tonnes, had a 3-metre-thick concrete base, and was surmounted by a 122-metre-high chimney. There was a shortage of skilled engineers for the project, and it was difficult to attract people to work in such a remote place.

'Cockcroft's Follies' are the square-shaped galleries around the tops of the chimneys.

Work went on round the clock in utmost secrecy. Housing for employees was provided, among other places, at Seascale, a seaside village with a golf course and two boarding schools. The in-comers formed a colony of highly-committed scientists and technicians.

A view of Seascale, on the coast of Cumbria, northwest England.

Working on the production of plutonium, Windscale, 1954. The gloves are set in holes in a lead glass screen.

The first reactor at Windscale began operating in October 1950, and the second in June 1951, though a series of government-imposed restrictions, known as 'D-notices', prevented news of the project and its purpose being reported. The two reactors contained thousands of uranium fuel cartridges packed in graphite. The uranium was bombarded with neutrons to set up a chain reaction in which the uranium was transformed into a number of different elements including plutonium – which does not exist in nature.

The plutonium was then extracted from the irradiated uranium fuel in a reprocessing plant known as B204. All the material used in this process becomes radioactive, so a large quantity of dangerous waste

'We knew if the Cold War situation had got worse ...'

Graham Harker worked at Windscale in the early days of plutonium production. He described the atmosphere:

'I was working on plutonium right from the start. At first it was all done by hand. We worked in special cabinets stirring up solutions of plutonium nitrate with a glass tube ... In those days producing plutonium came before anything else. We knew if the Cold War situation had got worse long before we heard it on the radio because up went the pressure to produce plutonium.' (Quoted in Cutler and Edwards, *Britain's Nuclear Nightmare*)

is left. At Windscale, highly radioactive waste was stored in huge steel vats; medium-level waste was stored in sludge tanks; and low-level waste was piped out through two 3-kilometre-long pipelines into the Irish Sea. The plutonium was sent to a secret military research centre at Aldermaston, to be incorporated in Britain's first atomic bomb.

The Soviet Union had tested its first nuclear device in 1949. Britain secured its position among the world powers in 1952, with a nuclear explosion in the Montebello Islands off the northwest coast of Australia.

October 1952: a three-kilometre-high cloud rises from the explosion of Britain's first nuclear device, in the Montebello Islands.

The first nuclear power stations

At Windscale, the huge amount of heat released by nuclear fission in the reactors simply disappeared up the chimneys. But it was realized that this was energy that could be harnessed to generate electricity.

Once Britain's bomb production programme was underway, and more plutonium was needed, it was decided to build four new reactors at Calder Hall, adjacent to Windscale, followed by four more at Chapelcross, in Dumfries. The purpose of all these new reactors was to convert uranium into plutonium for the British weapons programme. But the reactors would also be used to generate electricity for public use.

So it was that in 1956 Queen Elizabeth II travelled to Calder Hall to declare open the world's first nuclear power station. A Conservative government was in power and one of its leading members, R.A. Butler, accompanied the queen. A spirit of innovation and optimism pervaded the occasion. Press reporters did not ask questions about health and safety, nor about the growing stockpile of radioactive waste.

Opposite: Queen Elizabeth II at Calder Hall, the world's first nuclear power station, 17 October 1956.

How a nuclear power station works. The control rods are raised or lowered to control the rate of fission in the reactor.

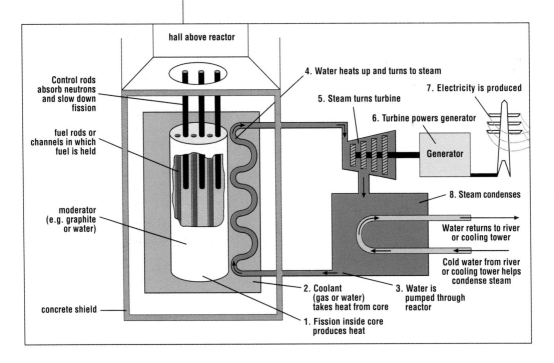

The threshold of a new age

On 17 October 1956 the world's first nuclear power station at Calder Hall, Cumbria, was officially opened by Queen Elizabeth II. Pressing a switch that sent nuclear-generated electricity into the power lines of northern England, she expressed feelings of both humility and pride:

'... all of us here know that we are present at the making of history. For many years now, we have been aware that atomic scientists, by a series of brilliant discoveries, have brought us to the threshold of a new age. We have also known that, on that threshold, mankind has reached a point of crisis. Today we are, in a sense, seeing a solution to that crisis as this new power, which has proved itself to be such a terrifying weapon of destruction, is harnessed for the first time for the common good ...

'We have been made vividly aware that the physical world ... is of a complexity which must inspire in us a sense of awe. More than that: in the atom, man has discovered vast powers and ways to control them, and their tremendous possibilities for good or evil must fill us with ... humility.

'As new fields open before us, we become conscious that a grave responsibility is placed upon all of us to see that man adds as much to his stature by the application of this new power as he has by its discovery. Future generations will judge us, above all else, by the way in which we use these limitless opportunities which providence has given us and to which we have unlocked the door ...

'For centuries past, visionary ideals and practical methods which have gone from our shores have opened up new ways of thought and modes of life for people in all parts of the world. It may well prove to have been among the greatest of our contributions to human welfare that we led the way in demonstrating the peaceful uses of this new source of power.

'I congratulate all those who have shared in this fine project ...'

Excitement

Some people were as excited by the changing of uranium into plutonium
as medieval alchemists had been when they dreamed of turning base metal
into gold. Some people foresaw nuclear-powered planes and cars.
As Britain struggled to emerge from wartime rationing and shortages,
some politicians spoke of electricity 'too cheap to meter'.

A culture of secrecy

In summer 1955, 'hot-spots' had been detected at
ground level around Windscale. Discharged fuel cans
were found to have been over-shooting and falling
into the air-ducts instead of into a skip as intended.
As their uranium oxidized, radioactive particles went
up the chimneys. This had been going on for two years.
The filters had failed to trap the particles. They were
also found to be torn. The new Atomic Energy
Authority, which in the same year took over
responsibility for both bomb-making and the nuclear
power programme from the Ministry of Supply, did
not make these facts public.

Calder Hall power station
photographed on the eve
of its opening by Queen
Elizabeth II. The dial would
show the amount of
electricity generated
when the queen pressed
the switch.

Among the press and
the public the wartime
spirit of loyalty, and of
everyone pulling together,
still existed in large
measure. The new
industry was tied to
weapons research and
Cold War definitions of
national security, so
anyone with expert
knowledge was sworn to
silence by the Official
Secrets Act. The nuclear
programme had therefore
been top-secret from the
start, and this culture of
secrecy continued.

FIRE AT WINDSCALE

The two reactors at Windscale had been built at great speed. The scientists and engineers involved were working at the cutting edge of nuclear physics, and took pride in their ability to improvise. One example was the belated decision to add filters to the chimney stacks. In 1957 these filters were put to a test for which they had not been designed. Reactor 1 was undergoing a procedure to release what was known as Wigner energy. This was energy that could build up in the graphite of the reactor, and which might be released spontaneously, with the danger of over-heating. The procedure, called an anneal, aimed to release the energy safely.

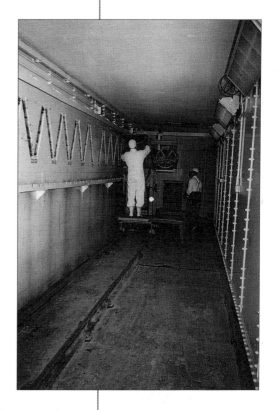

Inspecting the filters at the top of one of Windscale's chimney stacks, 1954.

On Monday, 7 October 1957, the anneal began. As the operators reduced the supply of cooling air in order to raise the temperature of the graphite, they needed to monitor variations in heat in other parts of the reactor. But the machinery to monitor such variations failed.

In the afternoon of Thursday, 10 October, there was a marked increase of radioactivity. The temperature in the reactor rose rapidly. As news got around, experts gathered in the control room. When the reactor core was inspected, four of the channels in which the fuel was held were seen to be red-hot. If the fire spread throughout the core, the results would be catastrophic.

It was decided to create a fire-break around the burning zone. A team of eight men with protective clothing, respirators and dosimeters, set about urgently pushing fuel cans out of the core with heavy steel bars.

A modern view of Windscale (renamed Sellafield). On the left are the cooling towers of the Calder Hall nuclear reactors. On the right is a nuclear fuel reprocessing plant. The globe-shaped building houses an Advanced Gas-cooled Reactor, now disused. The original reactors (left centre) were sealed and abandoned after the fire in 1957. In coming years the chimney stacks are to be dismantled.

From the roof, Tom Tuohy, deputy works manager, looked down through the inspection holes. Instead of dying down, the fire was spreading. All evening, a heroic attempt went ahead to try to eject more fuel cans. The men used every steel rod they could lay hands on, including scaffolding poles brought over from the Calder Hall construction site. But the cans were so distorted that it was hard to push them out. The steels rods came out red-hot and dripping with molten metal. At 1 a.m., a telephone call was made to the Chief Constable of the local police informing him of the emergency, while workers on the site were warned to stay indoors and to wear face-masks.

Through the early hours of Friday morning, efforts were made to control the fire. Carbon dioxide was pumped into the core, but to no effect. It had been decided to use water if all else failed, but this was a dangerous option because an explosion might result.

Four hoses were wired to poles ready to be pushed into the reactor above the fire zone. Eventually, just before 9 a.m., the water was turned on. To great relief, the critical moment passed and no explosion came. But the fire still burned strongly. Then it was decided to turn off the cooling fans, and quickly the fire began to die out. Around midday the Chief Constable was assured that the emergency was over and there would be no need for the evacuation of local people. Only then was a message sent to the Atomic Energy Authority in London.

Fire in Reactor 1

On Friday, 11 October, Sir Edwin Plowden, Chairman of the Atomic Energy Authority, received a brief message at his office in London:

'Windscale Pile No 1 found to be on fire in middle of lattice at 4.30 pm yesterday during Wigner release. Position been held all night but fire still fierce. Emission has not been very serious and hope to continue to hold this. Are now injecting water above fire and are watching results. Do not require help at present.' (Quoted in Arnold, *Windscale 1957*)

The hoses were left running for thirty hours, and by Saturday afternoon the reactor was cold. All the water had to be pumped into ponds on the site because it was highly radioactive.

Fall-out

From the afternoon of Thursday, 10 October, air samplers a kilometre or so from the factory recorded abnormal radioactivity. At first, a breeze carried the plume from the chimneys out to sea, but in the early hours of Friday morning the wind freshened and changed direction.

The first main release occurred around midnight on Thursday, when the uranium was burning. The second came on Friday morning, when water was put on the fire and a rush of steam went up the chimney stacks.

The result was that radioactive material was carried southeast over England, and eventually, in low concentrations, over Europe.

As the fire raged, no warning was given to local people. However, at least some of those who worked at Windscale put their families into cars and drove them out of the area before returning to help with the clean-up.

Cancers

When radiation comes into contact with a human cell, it damages it. If the cell survives in a damaged state, there is a danger that it can multiply inside the body, and cause cancer. If a person's reproductive organs are contaminated, then any children he or she conceives may be damaged too. Certain parts of the body are particularly vulnerable – especially in children.

No warning given

Dr Frank Leslie, a physicist who lived locally, wrote to the *Manchester Guardian* expressing his concern two days after the fire. His letter was published on 15 October 1957:

'Sir, As a Seascale resident I find it somewhat disquieting that there was no official warning to the public on Thursday and Friday that an abnormal amount of radioactivity, some of which was liable to fall on the village, was being released from the Windscale factory. Subsequent measurements in my garden have indicated that the beta-gamma fall-out amounted to twenty micro-curies a square metre, a value very much in excess of that resulting from normal factory operations and atomic bomb tests.

'In an incident of this kind, the course of which is quite unpredictable in its early stages, one would have thought that the Authority would have considered it prudent to warn people beyond the factory boundary to remain indoors. It is to be hoped that in any future incidents at this or any other factory or atomic power station the public will be better informed.'

'No danger now'

Ironically, between 8 and 26 October 1957, the *Sunday Times* and the UK Atomic Energy Authority were jointly staging an exhibition in London called 'Atom 1957'. On 13 October the paper reported 'an over-heating' in one of the reactors as a small item under the headline: 'Atom Pile: "No Danger Now"'. A spokeman for the UKAEA is quoted:

'Continuing measurements outside the site confirm there is no evidence of any increase in radioactivity which might have caused harm to the public.'

In 1957, it was known that radioactivity could reach humans through milk produced by cows grazing on contaminated pasture. Sure enough, tests on Saturday, 12 October, showed that milk collected the day before from local farms contained high levels of iodine 131 – a radioactive fission product that, if consumed, collects in the thyroid gland bringing the risk of thyroid cancer. But what level was dangerous? Previous estimates related only to the exposure of workers over their lifetime. No one had expected, or planned for, an emergency affecting the general population. No figures existed on the increased risk for infants, who have small thyroid glands, and drink a lot of milk.

Testing for radioactivity in the countryside around Windscale, 1958. A converted vacuum cleaner is used to take samples of air.

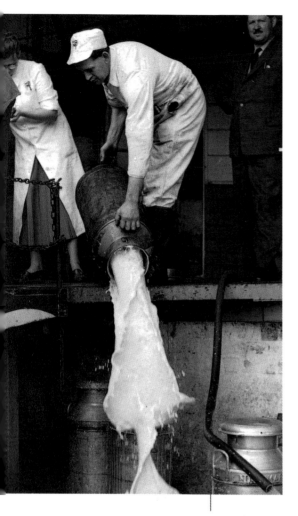

Huw Howells, Windscale's health and safety manager, telephoned atomic experts around the country, and quick calculations were made. As a result, on Saturday night, milk from 36.3 square kilometres around the nuclear plant – some 6,820 litres per day – was declared unsafe and banned from sale. When two days later the levels of contamination were found not to be falling as at first predicted, the milk ban was extended to a wider area, covering 518 square kilometres. All milk from this zone was poured away, though green vegetables and other produce were declared safe.

Inquiries

The AEA set up an internal board of inquiry, led by Sir William Penney. After ten days, it reported on mistakes made by staff, and deficiencies in the instruments they used. It highlighted under-staffing, and weaknesses in the way the Authority was organized.

Radioactive milk is poured away, 22 October 1957.

 The prime minister's dilemma

On 28 October 1957, Prime Minister Harold Macmillan was sent a copy of Sir William Penney's report into the fire at Windscale. He wrote on it, in red pencil:

'I have read all this, it is fascinating. The problem is two-fold.
a) What do we do? Not very difficult.
b) What do we say? Not easy.'

It recommended a full technical evaluation, and more thorough research. But the report was not widely read. For political reasons Prime Minister Harold Macmillan insisted that it should not be published; ministers and officials were ordered to hand in their copies, and the printer was required to surrender the proofs.

PLOWDEN   SIR WILLIAM PENNEY

To begin with, Windscale reactor 2 was kept in production. But over the following months more detailed reports revealed technical flaws that would be expensive to put right. Consequently, a year

At a press conference on Windscale, November 1957.

Plutonium and politics

Just a few days before he received the Penney Report, Prime Minister Macmillan had secured US President Dwight Eisenhower's agreement that he would ask Congress to allow scientific collaboration with Britain to resume. Britain had proved its ability to make atomic weapons, and was anxious to keep its place as a world power. For his part, Eisenhower was willing to cooperate. On 4 October the Soviet Union had launched the world's first space satellite, *Sputnik*, which raised fears that the Soviets might be overtaking the USA in advanced technology.

Although the Atomic Energy Authority was willing to publish the Penney Report, Macmillan insisted that it be kept secret. His diary entry for 30 October reveals why:

'The problem remains, how are we to deal with Sir W Penney's report? It has, of course, been prepared with scrupulous honesty and even ruthlessness. It is just such a report as the Board of a Company might expect to get. But to publish to the world (especially to the Americans) is another thing. The publication of the report, as it stands, might put in jeopardy our chance of getting Congress to agree to the President's proposal.'

Anti-nuclear protesters.

after the fire in Reactor 1, the prime minister announced that both Windscale reactors would be sealed and abandoned. Sir Christopher Hinton, chairman of the electricity board, said they would be a 'monument to our ignorance'. The new reactors at Calder Hall and Chapel Cross were not affected. As far as the general public was concerned, the accident was forgotten.

Radioactive fall-out

Cockcroft's Follies held back some of the contamination from the Windscale fire, but over the years that followed new estimates were made about how much radioactivity had been released. By the early 1980s, a number of radioactive substances had been listed which had not been mentioned before: iodine 131, caesium 137, strontium 89, strontium 90, tellurium 132, ruthenium 106, cerium 144, polonium 210 and titrium.

'Will this be part of the official history ...?'

Jenny Uglow was a pupil at the Calder Girls' School at the time of the fire. She wrote to the *Guardian* in 1987 – exactly thirty years later:

'Our daily walk was along the cinder track towards the power station; and we all drank the milk. On the night of the fire my father was fishing for sea-trout in the shadow of Windscale (he thought the men in the fields with torches were poachers!). A few years later my mother had severe thyroid problems and she was later operated on (successfully) for cancer. Next my father developed chronic, soon fatal kidney failure. We all know many, many people in the neighbourhood who have died young of cancer. Will this be part of the "official history", or do we have to tell our own? It has proven extremely difficult for ordinary people to contact the researchers: to whom should we submit the evidence?'

Evidence of the danger grows

Over time, more evidence came to light worldwide about the hazards of radiation. Research was not straightforward, since the human body may be subjected to radiation from several sources including sunlight, radon gas coming from the ground in certain geological areas, and medical X-rays. Dr Alice Stewart, concerned about an increase in childhood cancers since the war, discovered that they were more common where a child's mother had been X-rayed in pregnancy, proving the ill effects that relatively low levels of radiation can have, especially on a developing baby.

US researchers discovered that many people in Hiroshima when the bomb fell had absorbed lower doses of radiation than at first assumed, because they had been shielded by buildings. This meant that the illnesses they suffered must have been caused by lower levels of exposure than originally estimated.

In the USA, people living in Utah, Nevada and Arizona, states where nuclear weapons were tested through the 1950s and 1960s, were found to suffer a high incidence of leukaemia.

As evidence of the harmful effects of radiation grew, more people became involved in protests against the nuclear industry. In Cumbria, in 1995, people protest against a plan to dump radioactive waste underground.

THREE MILE ISLAND

The nuclear industry grew in size and confidence throughout the 1960s and 1970s. By 1979, more than 150 nuclear power stations had been built in 21 countries. The biggest concentrations were in the USA, Britain, the Soviet Union, France, Germany and Japan.

To begin with, only the first three of these nations possessed nuclear weapons. France joined them with its first nuclear weapons test in 1960; and, to international alarm, China followed suit with an explosion in 1964. In 1970 the United Nations Non-Proliferation Treaty came into force. It stated that nuclear weapons states would not transfer weapons to non-weapons states, and would not supply them with weapons-grade plutonium. Not all countries signed.

Types of nuclear reactors

Various types of reactor were built in different countries, in their search for the cheapest, safest and

Engineers at work in the core of a new reactor being developed at the Idaho National Engineering Laboratory.

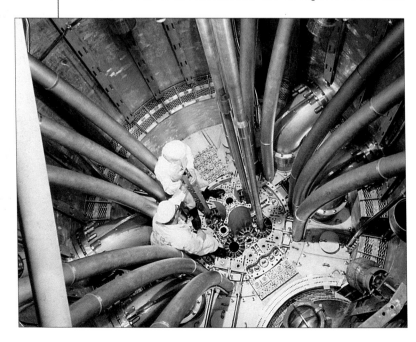

The turbine and generator at a nuclear power station in New Brunswick, Canada.

most reliable design. The USA and France developed pressurized water reactors (PWR), using water as both moderator and coolant. Reactors in Britain and the Soviet Union used graphite as the moderator. In the British Magnox and advanced gas-cooled reactors (AGR), the coolant was gas blown through the core, while the Soviet Chernobyl-type design used water as the coolant. France also developed power generation based on the fast breeder reactor: 'fast' because it has no moderator to slow the neutrons down; and 'breeder' because it produces plutonium, which, once reprocessed, can itself be used as a fuel.

In the USA, nuclear power plants were owned and run by commercial power companies. Overseeing the industry was a national organization called the Nuclear Regulatory Commission (NRC). Security at nuclear plants was a major concern, not least because of the danger of plutonium falling into enemy hands. The industry continued to be secretive. It was hostile to workers' organizations and to outside scrutiny.

Here, as in other countries, there were many incidents where health and safety were put at risk, but they were not made public.

Below: At a pressurized water reactor. The core is under many metres of water.

One of the most bizarre incidents occurred at Browns Ferry, Alabama, in 1975, when technicians searching for a leak in an electrical cable duct set fire to the cables with a candle. With luck and skill, the operators managed to shut down the reactors.

The Nugget File

Dr Stephen Hanauer, a senior official with the NRC, had the responsibility of reading reports on the operation of nuclear reactors in the USA. For ten years he hid details of the most unusual or worrying mishaps in a file he called the 'nugget file'. Under the USA's Freedom of Information Act, the Union of Concerned Scientists asked for permission to see the file. Otherwise its contents would have remained secret.

Karen Silkwood

Karen Silkwood was a 27-year-old employee at the Kerr-McGee plutonium factory, Oklahoma. Concerned about safety conditions within the plant, she became an active member of the Oil Chemical and Atomic Workers' Union (OCAW). While she was at work, she secretly collected evidence of how the company falsified data to cover up dangerous flaws in the welding of canisters containing plutonium. In turn, her employers asked the local police to keep her under surveillance.

On the evening of 13 November 1974, Karen Silkwood set out alone to drive to a meeting with an OCAW official and a reporter from the *New York Times*. Her folder of evidence was on the seat beside her. On the way, her car swerved off the road. Karen was found dead, and the folder mysteriously disappeared. At first, the police said she must have fallen asleep at the wheel, but investigation showed that her car had been pushed off the road. After extensive inquiries, in 1979 Kerr-McGee was fined $10 million for 'wanton and reckless' disregard for the safety of workers. No one has ever been prosecuted over Karen Silkwood's death.

Three Mile Island

The nuclear plant at Three Mile Island, a strip of land in the middle of the Susquehanna river in Pennsylvania, was owned by the Metropolitan Edison Company. In March 1979 it suffered the most serious accident in the history of the nuclear power industry in the USA.

The Three Mile Island nuclear power plant, Middletown, Pennsylvania.

Too-high temperatures in a reactor can cause 'meltdown': the fuel rods collapse into a molten mass. This could then burn through the reactor casing. Some people have said that it might burn right through the earth's core and emerge on the other side of the globe. From the USA, this would mean in China. That is why this scenario has been called 'The China Syndrome'.

On 16 March 1979 a Hollywood movie entitled *The China Syndrome* opened in New York and became a box-office hit. Based partly on the case of Karen Silkwood, it is a thriller about a faulty nuclear plant that goes out of control. The heroes are an honest employee and the television news crew who get the story out to the world, in spite of an attempted cover-up by the power company.

Less than two weeks later, fiction seemed to be turning into reality when reactor 2 at Three Mile Island (TMI 2) came close to disaster.

President Jimmy Carter (centre) and his wife visit the control room of Three Mile Island, 1979.

Shortly after 4 a. m. on Wednesday, 28 March, a series of faults occurred in the pump and valves of the reactor. As the operators tried to adjust matters, coolant water drained out of the reactor, and the top of the core was uncovered. It heated up to the point where the cladding on the fuel rods began to react and produce hydrogen. Some hydrogen escaped into the building in which the reactor was housed. Pumps began shaking violently, and the operators struggled to respond. At 1.50 p.m. a loud noise penetrated the control room. The hydrogen in the building had exploded. It was feared that the hydrogen bubble inside the reactor might explode next.

For five days TMI 2 hovered on the edge of catastrophe. The company issued reports that everything was under control. This was not true. Experts brought in by the Nuclear Regulatory

'I want to up-date our conversation ...'

The accident showed up a lack of coordination and emergency planning on the part of both the Metropolitan Edison Company (Met Ed) and government authorities. Public officials relied on news reports to find out what was happening. Local Mayor, Robert Reid, told how he telephoned Met Ed in the middle of Wednesday morning, 28 March 1979. He was assured that no radioactive particles had escaped and no one was injured.

'I felt relieved and relaxed; I said, "There's no problem." Twenty seconds later I walked out of my office and got in my car and turned the radio on and the announcer told me, over the radio, that there were radio-active particles released. Now, I said, "Gee whiz, what's going on here?" At 4.00 in the afternoon the same day the same man called me at home and said, "Mayor Reid, I want to update our conversation that we had at 11.00 a.m." I said, "Are you going to tell me that [radio-active] particles were released?" He said, "Yes."' (Quoted in *Report of the President's Commission*)

The human element

A Commission of Inquiry, chaired by John Kemmeny, published its report in October 1979. Only two of its 44 recommendations were connected with technical matters. The rest focused on a lack of direction in the industry, inadequate training of personnel, and a lack of concern for health and safety. Owners and operators of the plant at TMI were openly criticized.

'The most serious "mindset" is the preoccupation of everyone with the safety of equipment, resulting in the down-playing of the importance of the human element in nuclear power generation.'

Commission knew neither the extent of the accident, nor what to do about it. On the third morning, high levels of radioactivity were recorded above the plant.

Feeling unable to trust official assurances, many people drove out of the area. Press reporters, too, distrusted the company. Its conflicting statements only deepened everyone's anxiety. At midday on Friday, 30 March, Pennsylvania State Governor Richard Thornburg issued a recommendation that pregnant women and pre-school children should leave the area within an 8-kilometre radius of Three Mile Island. Officials scrambled to prepare for a full-scale evacuation of a 32-kilometre zone, involving 650,000 people, 13 hospitals and a prison. But the emergency was brought under control before these plans were put into operation. Late on Sunday afternoon the hydrogen bubble seemed to have grown smaller, and the danger of an explosion had passed.

Technicians enter the damaged reactor to take video tapes.

An anti-nuclear statement: 'Avoid self-destruction'.

A new movement

In the USA and in Europe a 'Green' movement had been gathering through the 1970s. Organizations such as Friends of the Earth and Greenpeace combined with local residents and conservation groups to make their voice heard in defence of the natural environment. Increasingly, they debated the issue of nuclear safety.

The nuclear debate

In 1979, the events at Three Mile Island were reported around the world. Many more people than before became concerned about the safety of nuclear power generation.

Those who argued for the industry said that it had a good safety record. Even though Three Mile Island had exposed problems, no one had been killed, and a disaster had been averted.

Protest succeeds

In Germany, in 1975, a proposal to build a nuclear power plant in Wyhl, on the Rhine, met with widespread opposition. 100,000 signatures were collected on a petition against the plant, and when work began felling trees to clear the site, protesters moved in. According to police reports, 28,000 demonstrators gathered along the banks of the river. Some had come from other countries in Europe. An organized group occupied the site, and stayed put for nine months.

On 15 March 1976, after hearing evidence from more than fifty experts, the Freiburg court issued its historic verdict:

'This unquantifiable risk, no matter how small, is unjustifiable when the enormous consequences of an accident are considered.' (Quoted in Bunyard, *Nuclear Britain*)

There was to be no reactor at Wyhl.

They pointed out that all forms of power generation have their draw-backs. Coal-mining is dangerous, and its waste tips spoil the countryside. The burning of fossil fuels creates acid rain. Oil spills from tankers at sea have polluted the water and coastline. Demand for electricity was growing fast worldwide. Only nuclear power could meet the demand cheaply and efficiently, especially in countries lacking coal or oil.

Those who argued against nuclear power pointed out that an accident in a nuclear plant could have not just regional but global consequences. Some nuclear waste would remain radioactive for thousands of years, leaving a hazardous legacy to future generations. Why did calculations of the cost of nuclear power not include the cost of waste disposal? Or cleaning up after accidents? Or de-commissioning nuclear reactors when they became too old? What about the danger of nuclear arms proliferation? They argued that conservation and alternative sources of power had been neglected. They said that growth should be sustainable rather than uncontrolled.

1989: workers at Three Mile Island manipulate remote-controlled robots in an area of the plant made radioactive by the accident.

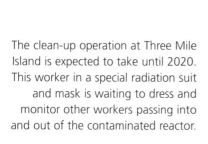

The clean-up operation at Three Mile Island is expected to take until 2020. This worker in a special radiation suit and mask is waiting to dress and monitor other workers passing into and out of the contaminated reactor.

ACCIDENTS AND THE MILITARY

The bombs dropped on Hiroshima and Nagasaki in 1945 remain the only nuclear bombs that have been exploded as an act of warfare. However, with enormous nuclear arsenals developed East and West in the half-century since then, many accidents occurred.

In 1965, a one-megaton nuclear bomb was lost in the Pacific, off Japan, when an A-4 warplane fell off a US Navy aircraft carrier. In 1966, a US Air Force B-52 bomber collided with a refuelling tanker in the air over Spain, killing its four-man crew. Two of its bombs detonated when they hit the ground. There was no nuclear explosion, but as plutonium in the bombs burned, the village of Polamares was contaminated with radioactive particles. The other two bombs were recovered from a river bed and the Mediterranean Sea. In 1968 another B-52 crash-landed in Thule, Greenland.

Crash landing

On 26 July 1956, a B-47 bomber crashed and caught fire while practising landings at the US Air Force base at Lakenheath, in East Anglia, England. The four men on board were killed. The plane's fuel caught fire, and flames spread towards an igloo-shaped bunker where nuclear warheads were stored, ready for the arming of bombs in case of war.

US service families three kilometres away were evacuated, and local people saw a convoy of vehicles leaving the base. They themselves were not warned of the danger. If the bunker had caught fire, a radioactive cloud would have drifted over East Anglia.

British security rules meant that details of this incident were withheld from public view for thirty years. The US authorities classified accidents involving nuclear weapons, in order of increasing severity, as Dull Swords, Bent Spears, or Broken Arrows. This one was classed as a Broken Arrow.

Activists on the Greenpeace ship *Rainbow Warrior* monitor pollution in the oceans. Sometimes they engage in direct action – entering nuclear test areas, or blocking nuclear waste discharge pipes.

All four bombs on board were ignited, contaminating the surrounding ice-cap. Most such accidents were kept secret, but some were brought to public attention by environmental campaigners.

Weapons testing

Gradually, more information came to light about the harmful effect of nuclear weapons testing both above and below ground. US servicemen who suffered ill-health after being made to witness test explosions fought for legal recognition of the harm done to them. Pacific islanders affected by test fall-out also waged a campaign for compensation.

Political leaders who believed in nuclear deterrence claimed that, in spite of the risks, nuclear weapons had the good effect of making another world war unthinkable. To that extent, they said, the arms race had succeeded in keeping the peace. However, though the Cold War ended, there was still great danger, particularly in countries such as Israel and Iraq, where nuclear weapons might be developed in secrecy.

Nevada, 1952: US Marines take part in an exercise involving an atomic explosion.

Nuclear-powered submarines

Nuclear submarines are powered by reactors on board. This means they can stay underwater for months at a time. The world's first was the US Navy's *Nautilus*, launched in 1954. Soon the USA, the Soviet Union and Britain had atomic fleets. All through the Cold War years, these submarines patrolled the northern oceans, playing a dangerous game of cat-and-mouse. They carried nuclear missiles, which could be launched at sea if hostilities broke out.

In 1963, the US nuclear submarine *Thresher* sank in the Atlantic and 129 lives were lost. The naval authorities denied that there was any danger from leaking radioactivity, though scorched debris suggested there had been a fire.

A Cruise missile rises from the Pacific after a test launch from a submarine.

A serious incident occurred in 1986, just days before US President Ronald Reagan and the Soviet leader Mikhail Gorbachev were to sign a nuclear test ban treaty. On 3 October 1986, the Soviet nuclear submarine K219 was within 1,600 kilometres of the east coast of the USA when a series of fires and explosions took place on board. Three men died as they tried to tackle the emergency. The submarine surfaced, its systems running out of control. As well as 16 missiles, a quantity of highly enriched uranium was on board. If an explosion occurred, a radioactive cloud could scatter fall-out on New York and Washington. US military bases were put on full alert.

Captain Britanov ordered a shut-down of the ship's reactors, but one reactor failed to respond. Two men climbed down into its chamber, into a temperature near boiling point. In radioactive steam, they struggled in vain to lower the control rods by hand, but emerged after half an hour, overcome by the heat.

Nautilus, the world's first nuclear submarine, on a visit to Portsmouth, England, 1961.

Knowing the danger, 19-year-old Sergei Preminin then went back into the reactor chamber and managed to shut down the reactor. But the door through which he must escape had been distorted by the heat and he died trapped inside. The rest of the crew were taken off K219 by Soviet freighters the next day, and the submarine was allowed to sink. Preminin was declared a Soviet hero and became known as 'the sailor who saved America'. Captain Britanov was dismissed from the navy, though cleared of blame for the accident.

The Soviet Navy lost other nuclear submarines in the Atlantic, the Sea of Japan and the Barents Sea. Some historians say that the true cause was the arms race, which pressed the Soviet Union to send poorly maintained vessels to sea and push them beyond their limits. Even when the arms race died down, the problem remained of what to do with old and dangerous nuclear submarines.

Kyshtym

Still shrouded in mystery is an accident which occurred in the late 1950s at the Soviet military installation of Kyshtym. When Zhores Medvedev, an exiled Soviet scientist, mentioned the catastrophe in the British magazine *New Scientist* in 1976, he was astonished to find that Western experts were unaware of it. Some accused him of trying to influence the debate about nuclear safety. Later the USA's Central Intelligence Agency revealed that it had long had evidence of a nuclear disaster in the region. Some people believe that Western governments hushed up the disaster because it revealed the danger of nuclear waste. As the policy of greater openness developed in the Soviet Union in the late 1980s, more information about Kyshtym came to light.

Kyshtym was a remote military installation where spent reactor fuel was reprocessed to make plutonium. At the time of the accident, waste had accumulated for several years. When an explosion took place, strontium-90 and caesium-137 were cast over a wide area. Hundreds of people were killed, and a comparison of old and new maps shows how the names of scores of towns and villages simply disappeared. A permanent exclusion zone, of about 1,000 square kilometres, still exists in the Chelyabinsk region of the Ural mountains.

A view of Hanford, c.1945 (see page 55). On the right is one of the reactors producing plutonium.

'It was like the moon'

Soviet scientist Lev Tumerman recalled driving through the Kyshtym region in 1960:

'As far as I could see was empty land. The land was dead – no villages, no towns, only chimneys of destroyed homes; no cultivated fields or pastures, no herds, no people – nothing. It was like the moon for many hundreds of square kilometres, useless and unproductive for a very long time, maybe hundreds of years.' (Quoted in Pringle and Spigelman, *The Nuclear Barons*)

A chronic event

Examining Hanford's record over four decades, Jack Geiger, medical professor at the City University of New York said in 1989:

'Chernobyl was an accident. Hanford was deliberate. Chernobyl was a singular event, the product of faulty reactor design and human error. Hanford was a chronic event, the product of obsessive secrecy and callous indifference to public health.' (Quoted in Shulman, *The Threat at Home*)

A hazardous legacy

The Hanford Reservation is a 1,450-square-kilometre area of Washington State, USA, where plutonium was made for the bomb dropped on Nagasaki. Military planners chose the remote location because of the nearby Columbia river, a ready supply of water to cool the reactors. They called Hanford a 'national sacrifice zone'. A new highway was built to enable speedy evacuation in case of emergency.

Between 1944 and 1956, Hanford released radioactive wastes into the environment 'on a scale that today would be considered a major nuclear accident', according to the *New York Times* forty years later. Some was released through poor filters, and some deliberately for experiment. Civilians living in the region were not warned.

Hanford is now one of the most contaminated regions on earth. When it ceased production in 1989, it had accumulated over 1,700 billion litres of liquid radioactive waste in leaky underground storage tanks. People living nearby have a high incidence of thyroid and other cancers. As recently as 14 May 1997, a chemical explosion in a storage tank blasted open the roof of one of eleven reactors standing idle on the site.

Tanks for storing liquid radioactive waste under construction at Hanford. Each tank would hold around 4 million litres.

WHAT NEXT?

Following the events at Three Mile Island in 1979, plans for many new nuclear plants in the USA, and in some other countries, were shelved while the industry reappraised the safety of reactor design and tried to improve its organization. The general public in many countries had been alerted to the dangers of nuclear power stations. The events at Chernobyl in 1986, when fall-out was detected across the northern hemisphere, made very clear that the consequences of a nuclear accident could be global.

In Britain, whether the nuclear industry laid plans to build a new reactor, dispose of waste, or reprocess more fuel, it was met at public inquiries with increasingly well-informed opposition. British Nuclear Fuels, formed to take over some of the functions of the Atomic Energy Authority in 1971, recognized the need to change its public profile and attempt to win over public opinion. In 1981 Windscale was renamed Sellafield, and in 1988 its high-tech visitors' centre opened.

A blue spruce tree in Ukraine, 1988. Its needles grow longer and lighter as a result of the accident at Chernobyl.

After Chernobyl

In the 1990s, following the break-up of the Soviet Union, it was difficult to continue monitoring the areas most contaminated by fall-out from Chernobyl. It was calculated that 70 per cent of the radionuclides had fallen on Belarus, now an independent country of some 10 million people; 20 per cent on Ukraine, also independent, in whose borders Chernobyl sits; and 10 per cent on what is now the Russian Republic.

A decade after the accident, vast tracts of forest, meadow and marshland remained contaminated. Caesium radionuclide concentrations in plants had not declined significantly. There was a big increase in thyroid and other cancers, especially among children. For example, in Belarus between 1986 and 1995 there were 390 cases of thyroid cancer in children up to age 14. Before the accident, only 5 cases per year had been recorded. There was also an increase in genetic disorders among the new-born. Millions of people suffered severe stress and depression.

Amidst the social and political dislocation of these years, dilapidated and poorly equipped hospitals struggled to provide treatment. Staff were sometimes not paid for months on end. Many children born with disabilities were abandoned into inadequate orphanages.

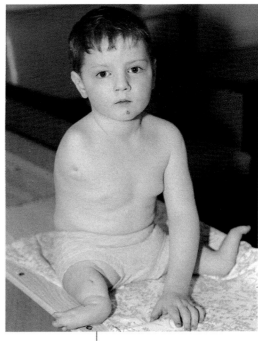

Conceived two months after the accident at Chernobyl, Igor was born with no right arm and tiny legs.

The exclusion zone around Chernobyl became a kind of bandit country where organized criminals stripped houses of radioactive timber to build homes on the Black Sea. Cooperation between the new states was not easy, and money was short. Charitable aid came from other parts of the world in the form of money, medicines and holidays for sick children.

In the late 1990s the Chernobyl power station is still operating. Here workers leave the plant at the end of the day.

Genetic mutations

During the 1990s, Swiss artist Cornelia Hesse-Honegger set out to document deformations occurring in insects with habitats close to Chernobyl, Sellafield (Windscale) and Three Mile Island. Because insects have a short life-cycle, it is possible to see hundreds of generations of insect within the normal lifespan of a human being. Her meticulous paintings document mutations already visible. She believes that in time mutations caused by nuclear fall-out will occur in other species, including humans. Some scientists say that her work is not conclusive evidence.

Opposite: Cornelia Hesse-Honegger's painting of a firebug larva that she found in Polesskoe, west of Chernobyl, in 1990. A section of the left feeler is missing.

International support as problems continue

The European Community (EC) funded projects to coordinate aid and research. One finding was that radioactivity had spread from highly affected to less affected areas through rivers and the draining of water through peat soils.

In 1997 the EC commissioner in charge of relations with eastern and central Europe, Hans van den Broek, announced that cracks had appeared in the sarcophagus built over Unit 4. There was a real risk that plutonium could escape. The international community had at that time sent $1 billion in aid to the region. He announced a further $100 million to renew the sarcophagus.

Shut-down at last?

Because of the economic crisis in Ukraine, other reactors at Chernobyl continued operating after the accident in Unit 4. It was hoped, though not certain, that they would be closed by the year 2000.

After nearly a half-century of nuclear power, even if no new reactors were to be built, all countries that have nuclear industries are faced with the need to manage and store radioactive waste, to clean up contaminated sites and plant, and to decommission nuclear reactors. All these processes involve safety risks. No one yet knows how costly they will prove.

DATE LIST

1932	The atom is split in the Cavendish Laboratory, Cambridge.
1939	
1 September	Hitler invades Poland, starting the Second World War.
1941	
7 December	Japanese aircraft attack the US naval base at Pearl Harbor. Britain and the USA declare war on Japan. In the Manhattan Project, US, Canadian and British scientists join to build a nuclear bomb.
1945	
7 May	Nazi Germany surrenders. In the Pacific, Japan fights on.
August	The US air force drops nuclear bombs on Hiroshima and Nagasaki. Japan accepts defeat.
1950s	Cold War weapons tests create low-level radioactive fall-out around the world. Servicemen are exposed to radiation to monitor the effect on their health and morale. Civil nuclear power develops in a culture of secrecy.
1952	Britain's first nuclear device explodes in the Montebello Islands, off Australia.
1956	
28 July	US air force B-47 crashes at Lakenheath, England, and fire spreads towards nuclear silos. Local people are not warned.

17 October	Queen Elizabeth II opens Calder Hall, the world's first nuclear power station.
1957	
10 October	Fire in reactor 1 at Windscale causes release of radioactive material, but local people are not warned. Contaminated milk is banned from sale.
1958	Nuclear waste explodes at a Soviet military facility, Kyshtym. This is kept secret.
1960-9	The Cold War intensifies.
1960	France begins nuclear weapons tests.
1963	US nuclear submarine *Thresher* sinks in the Atlantic.
1964	China begins weapons tests.
1970-9	Evidence grows of harmful effects of radiation. Anti-nuclear protest develops on an international scale.
1974	
13 November	Karen Silkwood is killed on her way to present evidence of safety violations at the Kerr-McGee plutonium plant in Oklahoma, USA.
1976	
15 March	A court in Freiburg, Germany, halts the building of a nuclear power station on the grounds of unquantifiable risk.

1979 28 March	Loss of coolant from the core of reactor 2 at Three Mile Island causes near disaster. The USA halts the expansion of nuclear power. The Soviet Union and France, heavily reliant on nuclear power, continue to build.
1986 26 April	Reactor 4 at Chernobyl explodes. For two days, local people are not warned.
28 April	Radiation is detected in Sweden and the Soviet Union is forced to admit the accident. A wide area is uninhabitable; contamination spreads across Europe.
9 May	With the fire out, the clean-up begins. By September the sarcophagus over Unit 4 has been built. Other units remain in production.

3 October	Soviet nuclear submarine K219 sinks in the Atlantic. Crew members give their lives to save the USA from radiation disaster.
1988	Sellafield (formerly Windscale) opens a visitors' centre to improve the nuclear industry's image and reassure the public.
1991	The Soviet Union breaks up. Ukraine and Belarus struggle to cope with the continuing ill health and early death caused by the accident at Chernobyl.
1997	The European Community reports on cracks in the sarcophagus and pledges aid for its renewal. It is hoped to close the Chernobyl power station by the year 2000.

RESOURCES

RECOMMENDED READING

Lorna Arnold, *Windscale 1957, Anatomy of a Nuclear Accident*, Macmillan Academic and Professional Ltd, 1992

Catherine Caufield, *Multiple Exposures, Chronicles of the radiation age*, Penguin, 1990

James Cutler and Rob Edwards, *Britain's Nuclear Nightmare*, Sphere Books, 1988

Peter King, *Nuclear Power: the facts and the debate*, Quiller Press, 1990

Piers Paul Read, *Ablaze, The Story of Chernobyl*, Secker & Warburg, 1993

Report of the President's Commission on the Accident at Three Mile Island, Pergamon Press, 1979

Adi Roche, *Children of Chernobyl: the human cost of the world's first nuclear disaster*, Fount Paperbacks (HarperCollins), 1996

FILMS

The China Syndrome is a thriller about a US power company that falsifies evidence of faults in the construction of a nuclear power station. *Silkwood* is based on the life and death of Karen Silkwood (see page 44).

MUSIC

Musicians United for Safe Energy (MUSE) organized 'No Nukes' concerts at Madison Square Garden, New York, 1979. There is a triple album with a ten-page insert.

GLOSSARY

atom, splitting the atom   Atoms are the basic building blocks of all substances. Locked into the nucleus of the atom is tremendous energy. When bombarded with neutrons, the nucleus splits, releasing energy and more neutrons; these then bombard other nuclei, thus setting up a chain reaction.

Communist Party   The Communist Party held power in the Soviet Union from the Bolshevik revolution in 1917 until 1991. The Soviet Union was run as a one-party state. Individuals could not succeed in any field of endeavour – including industry and science – without the support of the party.

control rods   rods that enable the level of power of a reactor to be held constant or varied as required. They are usually made of steel and contain boron or cadmium which can absorb neutrons. Lowering the control rods into the core of the reactor reduces fission and thus reduces power.

coolant   a gas or liquid circulated through the core of a reactor in order to extract heat released in the process of fission.

core   the central part of a reactor, containing the fissile material (material that is to undergo fission).

European Community (EC)   (formerly a group of 6 countries known as the Common Market, later expanding to become the European Economic Community) an organization of 15 member countries in Europe, working for economic and political cooperation. The EC is led by a Council of (national) Ministers and a directly elected European Parliament.

fuel can   container into which fuel in the form of rods or pellets is inserted and sealed to prevent leakage into the coolant.

genetic damage   Radiation can damage all cells in the body, including those involved in reproduction. The damage may be handed on to succeeding generations in the form of physical and mental impairment.

iodine   Iodine collects in the human thyroid gland. Radioactive iodine 131 can cause thyroid cancer. When there is a risk of exposure, taking iodine pills will fill the thyroid gland so that it does not take up radioactive iodine.

leukaemia   cancer affecting the blood cells.

Manchester Guardian   the former name of *The Guardian*.

plutonium   a heavy, highly radioactive metallic element which does not exist in nature. It is made artificially in reactors from the fission of uranium.

reactor   a device designed to initiate and control a chain reaction in fissile material.

thyroid   a gland in the neck which plays a key part in the functioning of various bodily systems, including the brain.

uranium   a heavy, radioactive metallic element mined in various parts of the world and used as fuel in nuclear reactors.

INDEX

SOURCES

The quotations in this book were taken from:
Lorna Arnold, *Windscale 1957, Anatomy of a Nuclear Accident*, Macmillan Academic and Professional Ltd, 1992; Gill and Macmillan Ltd, Dublin, 1992
Peter Bunyard, *Nuclear Britain*, New English Library, London, 1981
Children of Chernobyl (TV documentary), Yorkshire Television/Channel 4
James Cutler and Rob Edwards, *Britain's Nuclear Nightmare*, Sphere Books, 1988
Mikhail Gorbachev, *Memoirs*, Doubleday, 1995
Zhores A. Medvedev, *The Legacy of Chernobyl*, Basil Blackwell, 1990

Peter Pringle and James Spigelman, *The Nuclear Barons*, Michael Joseph, 1982; Sphere Books, 1983
Piers Paul Read, *Ablaze, The Story of Chernobyl*, Secker & Warburg, London, 1993
Report of the President's Commission on the Accident at Three Mile Island, Pergamon Press, 1979
Adi Roche, *Children of Chernobyl: the human cost of the world's first nuclear disaster*, Fount Paperbacks (HarperCollins), 1996
Seth Shulman, *The Threat at Home, Confronting the toxic legacy of the US military*, Beacon Press, Boston, 1992